PETER DEWAR

Overcoming Depression: A Real-Life Guide to Healing

Your guide to reclaiming peace and purpose

REFLECT PRODUCTIONS

For all of those who have suffered alone, when you want to give up in your darkest hours — this book is for you.
My family and friends who have buoyed me through every storm. And to those courageous souls just starting the path of becoming whole once again, I hope that you find a way to take back your life and trust in the goodness that lies in store for you down the road. This is for your endurance, your evolution and every ounce of happiness you should have.

"You see, you wouldn't ask why the rose that grew from the concrete had damaged petals. On the contrary, we would all celebrate its tenacity, we would all love its will to reach the sun"

- TUPAC SHAKUR

Contents

Foreword

There is no journey more personal than that of battling depression. The road is not a straight line, yet surely not the easiest. This book was written because of my own challenges, victories and learning through directly tackling depression. I understand the pain, the numbness, the aloneness and the struggle that is faced every single day.

Initially when I began writing this book, I intended to make it more than a guide. I desired to write to a friend — someone who goes along the journey with you, but provides not only tangible resources and techniques, but also support and encouragement. It is a guide on how to go from the depths of uncertainty and despair to lightness, purpose, happiness.

You will find the tools that worked for me throughout the chapters, and those supported by science and practice. Now, every section is created to give you knowledge but also empower you to do — even if that may feel like the tiniest of steps at first. Please feel free to take from this what you will, and pace yourself on your journey integrating those aspects which are most relevant and pertinent to your experiences.

It's time to start. For those of you who are just now beginning to grasp what depression is, or for those who have been battling it for years — this book is for you. There is hope, and there are solutions. You deserve to live life outside of depression — you should experience joy, meaning, and peace.

Thank you for sharing this journey with me. This book can help you get there, follow the light, out of that dying dark situation.

Hugs to you,

Peter

Preface

When I sat down to write this book, my main aim was a simple one: to be of use to others who are going through, as I did, episodes of depression so great that it was impossible to understand how they could ever end. I know what it can be like, the soul-destroying depths that one falls to within depression, how alone you feel and the complete lack of a starting point to get better.

This book is my own journey turned into lessons. A few of the strategies, insights, and tools that saw me through depression. I wrote this book because I believe wholeheartedly in recovery—no matter how impossible it feels sometimes.

Depression tends to shrink your world and make you feel like you have fewer choices. Today though, I am here to tell you that there is hope and ways to heal.

If anything, this book is an accompaniment. This isn't a read it once book, but one that you can go back to when in need of direction or comfort. Recovering from depression is a roller coaster and relapses happen. But with patience, perseverance and some helpful tools you can take little steps to rediscover yourself again.

In reading these pages, you will receive guidance and tips as well as feel supported and encouraged. Remember, every little step towards healing contributes something important to your overall recovery. Invest in yourself as you will bring happiness and fulfilment back into your life.

Thank you for letting me share this journey with you.

With gratitude and hope,

Peter

Acknowledgments

It has been a journey that would not have been possible without the generosity and sacrifices of so many people who helped me write this book in so many ways.

To my family, who have been the support and strength. Your faith in me — your unwavering faith, even at my lowest points— has been invaluable. Thank you for being so patient, loving and caring with me through all of this.

Friends who have been there for me, the kind words spoken when they were most needed. You have been so instrumental in this healing process.

I also want to specifically thank the mental health professionals whose expertise helped me through my tough times. You do important and life-changing work, and I hope that this book will be a testament of the efforts you put in every day to make a positive impact in others' lives.

And finally, to all the depression and mental health sufferers out there, this book is for you too. Finding your strength to reach out, to fight and to keep going. I trust this book will remind you that you are not alone, and a perfect world where only love, healing and happiness exists is just around the corner.

With deep appreciation,

Peter

Prologue

Rolling out of bed used to be the toughest challenge of any day — when every inhale felt like a chore and every thought, a burden. Despondency isn't just melancholy or a flicker, it's a burden that remains, frequently imperceptible to other people yet always obvious to the individuals who bear it. I went far too long never knowing how it was possible for the world to move and yet I could not because somewhere inside my heart things had fallen apart then torn apart and then finally ripped open.

The thing that no one tells you about depression is how isolating it really is. You could be sitting in a room full of strangers, surrounded by friends, family or colleagues and yet here you are at the same time feeling so incredibly isolated. You want to get help, but the words never form to come out right. You tell yourself that you are alone, and nobody would understand, or worse none would care.

Eventually, you find yourself at a crossroad where standing still is an unacceptable choice. That little flicker was no big light bulb moment or dramatic change in the tide for me. It was subtle—an unassuming moment where I became aware that indeed there lay a choice, and it was my own; to continue in the shadowlands of my mind, or simply take one single step forward to become happier. Taking that first step was the most difficult, but also the most necessary.

This book is about making that move, it is the courage to face those parts of you that are shattered, then push through the urge to crawl back into yourself as if it were your ship on stormy seas instead of a sinking anchor. I am not here to tell you that the journey is easy or there is a quick fix. Healing from depression is neither of those things. And I so wish that I could give you that but what I can promise you is there is a path ahead of you — one which leads to not just survival but better yet — to true and real life full of purpose and life.

You have just taken your first step by deciding to read this book. I wrote these pages to be with you on your path—not as a guide but as a companion. We will investigate the tools, mental shifts and emotional reinforcement to support you through the darkness into light together. It's not easy, but I swear to you — it is worth every ounce of effort you put into it.

Remember as you read: You are not alone in this battle. Even when it feels like the darkness is endless, there is hope. There are brighter days coming, this is where it starts.

With understanding and hope,

Peter

Introduction

Depression is not just a word for feeling sad. This burden makes daily life feel heavy and unbearable. If you have this book in your hands, it is probably because the burden on your heart has been too heavy, and you are searching for some light. The good news is, you are not alone, and help is available. Here's a step-by-step guide to help you on your journey to the light.

First place to start is with the recognition of what depression is.

You cannot just snap your fingers and turn it off or positivity train wreck-through it (make a point about how positive thinking is not the answer either). Depression is a reality; it affects every aspect of your life. But identifying them is a big win. You are so much more than your depression but welcome the suffering as it is the beginning of some resolve.

Recovery is not like a light switch. It is a process, and that is perfectly fine. You may be uncomfortable or completely unprepared to do this, but the main thing is that you take a small step forward in life. This book lays out practical simple steps you can take every day to get your feel-good vibes back. It is like building a house — you must start with a solid base for it not to collapse. For you, perhaps that foundation looks like establishing other habits to recognise and discuss your emotions and to weather the challenging times.

Recovery is about taking solid measured steps. Small habits will work to unshackle depression from your brain and guide you on the path to a fuller existence.

You do not need to handle this alone. Asking for help is brave. Opening up to a friend, family member or a professional can be the difference between life and death. You may feel alone in this but know that there are people out there who truly do care and who want you to get through this.

Asking for support is not about being weak; it means opening yourself up to the resources you need to heal.

Healing is an ever-going thing and there is no fixed method of doing it. Each small step is progress. The fact that you are here takes courage and it is a step in the right direction, and you should be proud of yourself. Recovery is possible, and you can lead a life of the person who deserves healing. Allow me to take you down that road, one step at a time.

Chapter 1: Understanding the Nature of Depression

D epression is often misunderstood as feeling sad, but it is
so much more than that. It's a mental health condition
that can affect almost every aspect of your life, from your

emotions to your physical health. In this section we will look at what depression is, what causes it and identify its triggers, so that you can begin your recovery process with clarity.

What is Depression?

Depression affects how you feel, think and behave, often making it hard to carry out daily activities. It's not simply a case of feeling a bit down for two or three days — it is a long-term condition which can last weeks, months or even longer.

Emotional symptoms

Depression can make you feel persistently sad or empty. You may have a sense of hopelessness and think that nothing will ever get better. People with depression often feel distanced from others, deprived of every master and it is as though life has lost its zest. For example, you used to love meeting friends and are now at best indifferent to such gatherings or simply burdened by the thought of them. This could well be an indication of depression.

Practical Tip: Begin to keep a diary of your mood. Every day, write down how you feel emotionally. This can help you notice trends and see if your feelings of despair or emptiness are ever-present.

Physical symptoms

Many people are surprised to discover that depression can cause physical symptoms such as constant fatigue or changes in appetite. Some people overeat for solace, while others may lose their appetite altogether. Some people also have sleep disturbances: you either have trouble falling asleep or sleep too much.

Practical Tip: Pay attention to how your body is changing. Are you sleeping more than usual? Do you feel exhausted even though you're resting? Have you noticed any differences in your eating habits? Understanding these patterns is an important step in realising your depression.

Cognitive symptoms

Depression often makes it difficult for you to think clearly. It is difficult to concentrate and make decisions.

Practical Tip: Start practising "thought challenging." Write down your negative thoughts and ask yourself if they are 100% true or not. What evidence do I have that opposes this thought? Over time, this simple exercise can lead to a shift in perspective. (Go on, give it a go- what have you got to lose?)

One important difference between depression and normal sadness is in the extent and duration of the sadness. Ordinary sadness comes and goes; typical sad feelings are triggered by specific events. But depression does not. It hangs around, permeates into every part of your life. When you find yourself hardly able to get out of bed in the morning for lack of energy or don't feel like going to work at all because things seem so hellish, you're likely experiencing something more than just "the winter blues."

Another key difference is that depression affects how you see yourself. You may develop a persistent negative self-image — feeling constantly and without let-up that you are worthless, or a burden on your friends and family members... even though such feelings do not accurately reflect reality.

Practical Tip: Share your feelings with someone you trust. Talking about how you are feeling can be the first step toward breaking out of a cycle of isolation and negative self-talk.

Common Myths and Misunderstandings

There are many misunderstandings about depression, and this can make it harder to seek help or make people understand.

'It's just in your head.' This myth implies that depression is not a serious medical illness but rather some kind of emotional distress or mental weakness on the part of those who suffer from it. In fact, however, depression is a genuine medical condition of the brain, much like heart disease or diabetes. It is not simply an attitude or mood which can be changed by an act of will. The number of times when I have heard people say, 'Just snap out of it.' Depression doesn't go away just because you want to feel better. It takes effort, often including professional help, changes in lifestyle and time.

With no professional help: A lot of people think that handling depression themselves is the best thing. But seeking professional help is not weak–it's smart. Why? Because if you had a fever or cough, you'd see a doctor just to get the right treatment. So too for your mental health, it's important to be supported.

Try getting in touch with Wellbeing, you'll be surprised at how much support there is out there https://www.wellbeingnands.co.uk

Identify Triggers and Underlying Causes

One of the most empowering things you can do in your recovery is to see what's triggering your depression. Once you know the reasons, you can start managing and reducing their impact on your life.

Genetic and Biological Factors

Does depression run in your family? If a close relative has suffered from depression, you may have a much higher risk of getting it too. This doesn't mean, however, that all your children are doomed to suffer as a result.

Imbalances in brain chemistry

Serotonin and dopamine are two of the mood regulating neurotransmitters. If these chemicals are out of balance, they can drag you into depression.

Hormonal and medical conditions

Hormonal changes can trigger depression, such as those during menstruation. In addition, medical conditions like thyroid diseases or long-term pain disorders may also contribute to depressive symptoms.

Tip: If you think that a medical condition may be having an active influence on your mood, ask your doctor for a physical examination. A crucial element in getting well is identifying any underlying medical problems.

Environmental Influences

Major life changes may well precipitate depressive symptoms. It could happen after losing a job, going through some trauma, or making a change in one's living arrangement. Even big moves or marriage can be trying enough to tip you over into depression.

Isolation and relations

Depression isolates people: in turn, isolation only serves to make it worse. An unstable romantic relationship or other strained relations with one's family or friends can also be counted as factors.

Socioeconomic factors and pressures

Financial problems, work pressures and social pressures are all virtually inevitable going to give rise to people's depression rates if those problems persist.

One Useful Tip: Pick out a currently stressful area in your life that you can do something about and come up with an achievable small step towards lessening the pressure. For example, if you find work overwhelming, could you delegate one of the tasks or set stricter boundaries there?

Psychological Patterns

Negative thinking and self-blame. Depression feeds back on itself, and harsh talk or patterns of thinking can take root. For instance, someone with depression might and often will tell themselves (negative self-talk), "I'm a loser," or "I'll never get any good."

Cognitive distortions

Re-labelling and arbitrary inferences; all-or-nothing thinking, which is so often associated with depression.

Suffering from past traumas and unresolved sad memories

Unresolved old issues can feed into persistent feelings of despair. It might be childhood trauma or grief over a loss.

One Useful Tip: When negative thoughts appear, try using mindfulness techniques. Just observe the thought without making any judgement about it at all. Try to know it is there, and then let it go by itself rather than engage with that thought.

Recovery from depression is neither quick nor easy. There are lots of twists and turns along the way and setbacks to serve as setbacks. But through time, effort and the appropriate tools recovery is possible. Here's why:

Recovery is Non-Linear

There may be days when it feels like you've made great progress and others with nothing at all. That's natural. Recovery is seldom a straight line—it's more like a wave, with ups and downs. What is important though is to concentrate on moving forward even if it moves slowly.

Practical Tip: Whenever something goes wrong, tell yourself it's all part of the process. And when you are feeling down

11

or facing a slump in mood, remember those little victories—however short-lived they might be such as getting out of bed or going for some fresh air.

Facing Emotional Challenges

One of the most difficult aspects of the process of recovery is enduring uncomfortable emotions. Depression often persuades you to avoid or suppress your feelings, but part of recovery is allowing yourself to experience painful emotions and hear them out without judgement. It's okay to be vulnerable, and it's okay to ask others for help when you need it.

Participate: Create a self-care plan that includes things like breathing exercises or spending time with good friends

Building Hope and Resilience

Hope is one of the most important factors in recovery. Even when it seems dim, reminding yourself that recovery is possible can give you a little more motivation. Just because a person is resilient doesn't mean they won't run into any difficult times. The difference is that when or if they do face tough times, they have the resources and support needed to get through.

Practical Tip: Write down whatever happy thing is coming your way, no matter how small. Post it somewhere you'll see it so it can remind you that little flames of hope can grow into a fire.

Recovery from depression is possible, even if it feels like it isn't right

now. *Recognising what depression is, what triggers it, and that healing takes time can set you on the right path towards a brighter future. By getting this far (i.e. reading this), you have made a good start already. It's time to continue from here—just one step at a time.*

2

Chapter 2: Building the Foundation for Recovery

P *reparing to overcome depression involves these key steps: You must accept and acknowledge your depression; And create a plan that is tailored for you, so thereby grow from within; Then gradually add small habits—some feasible and some easy to do—which will maintain your mental balance.*

The Power of Acceptance

The first, hardest but most necessary step in recovery is acknowledging that one is indeed faced with depression. The sound of that might be simple, but many people find it hard to do. Acknowledging sickness in oneself makes guilt or shame stand out, and because most individuals have enough of these feelings already this is a difficult task. Acceptance of your emotions is not an admission of failure, but rather your first brave step towards recovery. Having accepted what's happening, you can focus on solving problems and stop banging your head against the wall trying to get rid of anxiety and depression. Acceptance enables you to see yourself in a different light, to look at your difficulties more objectively than ever before.

Actionable Tip: Write down your feelings. Keep a diary in which you honestly note your feelings, thoughts, and any physical symptoms present. This will help externalise your struggles and perhaps give them perspective.

Why Acceptance is the First Step to Change

Fighting against emotions usually makes them stronger, creating additional worries and perhaps even sleepless nights. Furthermore, when you accept your struggle it's like giving yourself permission to start taking care of needs you've been ignoring all along—and without this acceptance things hanging over from before just tend not to be dealt with at all.

Practical Tip: Nowadays, the concept of acceptance, which is also reflected in practising mindfulness, seems to be gaining ground. Dedicate a few minutes each day to simply be present with your own sensations and not attempt to alter them—just let them be. Be aware of the thoughts and feelings passing through you, without trying to excuse them with lines like "I shouldn't feel this" or other reductive judgments such as that one.

Receiving Self-Compassion with Every Mental Health Struggle

When we are struggling with depression, we are used to severely judging ourselves, but this habit only serves to make our emotional pain worse. If it is when you are gentle with yourself, that is creating a healing vestige.

Effective Suggestion: When negative self-talk comes up, pause for a moment and ask yourself, "Would I speak to a friend who's always struggling this way?" If not, then change the things you say to things which are kind. Instead of saying "I'm too weak," for example, change it into something like "I am having a rough day and that is all right."

How to Let Go of Denial and Guilt

For many people a sense of guilt or shame accompanies their depression: they blame themselves for feeling this way. But here's the bottom line: Depression isn't your fault. It's not something you've done wrong or brought on yourself. It's a medical condition that needs to be attended to and treated. Let go of denial and guilt so you have the energy for recovery.

Effective Suggestion: Spend 10 minutes writing out any sense of guilt, shame, or self-blame which exists inside yourself. Then next to each statement, write out a more compassionate alternative statement (e.g., instead of "I'm falling short" write "I am going through hard times and that's okay").

Overcoming Social Stereotypes and Self-Review

When you think you are "weak" for being depressed, or that you ought to be able to handle it on your own–this kind of self-revulsion has an internal and external origin. However, remember that depression is something that can be treated or healed; it will not show this characteristic for long. One component of overcoming social stereotypes is learning that all mental health struggles are normal, and it is a strong thing to ask for assistance.

Tip: Speak to someone who trusts what you're going through. If you share your struggles with someone who is supportive, it can break down the barriers that shame and isolation are trying to create for you.

Working to Overcome Internalised Stigma

Society's view of mental health is easily absorbed; so much that many people internalise their depression. This internalisation makes us think that depression should be hidden away rather than out in the open. To accept and transform these ideas is essential for starting off on a pathway toward peace.

Actionable Tip: The next time you have a negative thought about your depression, take it head-on. Question where it sprang from and whether those thoughts are truly useful or actually accurate. State factual responses: "Depression is something that exists, not a defect. It's natural to ask for help in dealing with such a condition."

Countering the Social Judgments

Societal attitudes toward depression can create actual hindrance in seeking help. Just as with any other disease, there should be no shame attached to receiving treatment for depression.

Actionable Tip: Learn about living with depression as a treatable condition to survive—Reading literature from mental health institutions, books, or getting in touch with support groups will for sure provide fresh insights into what this kind of compassionate disease really means.

Developing a New Way of Looking at Depression

It is most important to recognise that, no matter where you are, depression while hard is indeed curable, nevertheless. It is not a state that one stays in forever and many people have indeed conquered their depression through some combination of therapy, medication and lifestyle changes.

Tip: Research the success stories of people who have beaten depression. Knowing that a cure is possible can give you confidence to ask for help and keep going.

Establish a Support Network

Sharing your story with a couple of friends or family members is in fact the first step to recovery from depression. A support group will help you feel less alone and open the doors for help.

Actionable Tip: Start by sharing with someone you feel you trust how you're feeling. Be straightforward about your experience and tell them what they can do to help you out, whether that is just listening or helping with some daily tasks.

Finding Professional Help

Therapists, counsellors and mental health professionals have training and experience with recovery. Therapy can supply you with coping strategies, emotional support, and fresh views on dealing with depression.

Actionable Tip: Research online therapy options or local mental health professionals. Make a list of therapists so you can make an appointment to have an initial consultation as the first step. You can also ask your doctor for help if you're not sure where to start.

Identifying Personal Goals for Recovery

Recovery looks different for everyone, which is why it's essential that you decide what the process means to you. Start with identifying both short-term and long-term goals. For example, short-term goals might be things like cutting down on negativity or just by brushing your teeth. Long-term goals would concentrate more on creating a life filled with joy and contentment.

Actionable Tip: Write down two short-term goals and two long-term goals. Make sure they are clear and achievable (e.g., "I want to spend 15 minutes a day applying mindfulness" or "I want to enrich the relationships in my life").

Setting Realistic and Attainable Milestones

Recovery can seem daunting, but breaking it up into smaller, manageable steps makes feelings of achievement more likely. Instead of aiming for immediate, drastic changes, think about small, regular increments.

Actionable Tip: Break your goals into small steps. For instance, if one of your goals is to improve your mood, start with something like "Practise gratitude for five minutes each morning". Keep a record to monitor how far you've come over time.

There are many strategies for dealing with depression, from cognitive-behavioural therapy to meditation. So, it is essential that you study different approaches to see what fits best for your own case.

Actionable Tip: Pick one new therapeutic method like CBT or mindfulness meditation. Spend a week trying it out and see how you feel afterwards. You may have to try a few methods before something clicks for you.

Staying on Track and Adjusting Strategies

Regularly review and adjust your daily plan. As you review your progress, you may find that a little tinkering here and there will make all the difference.

Actionable Tip: Record your daily mood in a diary or use a mental health tracking app. Regularly check back over what progress you have made, and test whether things need to be amended.

Health and Depression

Caring for your physical self is an essential part of treating depression. Regular exercise, good eating habits, and quality sleep can be just the fix for what's dragging you down.

Actionable Tip: Start with five minutes of physical activity once a day. It could be as simple as a little stretching, walking round the park, or a few gentle yoga poses. Steadily increase the time as you feel more comfortable.

Nutrition and Mental Health

What you eat can affect your mood and energy. A balanced diet can bring more calm to your temperament and add to your overall physical well-being.

Actionable Tip: Pay more notice to fruit, vegetables and whole foods in general from now on. Begin with something small: Perhaps just swap out one sweet snack for a healthier alternative daily.

Sleep Hygiene Tips for A Better Night's Rest

Quality sleep is essential to good mental health. Building a sleep routine can help you feel more rested and alleviate symptoms of depression.

Actionable Tip: Pick a time for sleep that works best with the way your life flows and, since rest should be calm and peaceful, give yourself some form of pre-sleep relaxation such as reading aloud or doing relaxation exercises. Nice hot bath. Lavender spray on the pillow. Try an hour of no computer screen time before bed instead. It might just give your sleep quality a shot in the arm!

Building a Routine

Structure can give you a sense of order, especially when you are feeling overwhelmed. Even a very simple routine will make things seem more routine and so less strange than they might do after reading this far.

Actionable Tip: Make it a habit to plan your day the night before. Start with simple tasks such as "Make the bed" or "Drink a glass of warm water in the morning." Gradually, as your routine becomes habit-forming and natural, you can add in more detail.

Including Self-Care Activities

Self-care is an essential part of recovery, not just a luxury. Make time for yourself to reduce stress and avert burnout.

Actionable Tip: Set aside at least 15 minutes each day that you can do something you enjoy, whether it is reading, taking a bath or listening to music. Treat this time like any other important appointment or commitment.

Maintaining Energy Levels and Preventing Burnout

While you are recovering, it is important not to push yourself too hard. Burnout will only make depression worse.

Actionable Tip: Make a point of keeping track of your energy levels. When a feeling of increasing fatigue sets in, take some time to rest. Learn how to say 'no' when tasks and responsibilities feel too heavy or overwhelming.

Preparing for recovery means facing where you are, making a plan that fits your life, and taking small yet vital steps. These aren't intended to be perfect; they are intended to lead you step by step. You are already charting a course towards recovery, and every step made brings you closer to life that's more abundant and healthier. Keep

23

going– one tiny action at a time.

3

Chapter 3: Managing Thoughts and Emotions

The way you talk to yourself has a direct impact on how you feel and act. Often our internal dialogue becomes filled with negative, automatic thoughts that help stoke a sense of depression. However, with the right tools you can carry this dialogue into something constructive and empowering.

Recognising Negative Self-Talk

Some negative self-talk comes so quickly that we hardly even notice it. But paying attention is the beginning of ending this behaviour.

Tip: Keep a thought journal. Record each negative thought you notice during your day. Record these critical or pessimistic statements in a notebook or app, in this way you become conscious of your tendencies.

Tip: Learn to recognise critical words. When you find yourself using words such as "always," "never" or "should," these often signal unrealistic or unproductive thinking patterns and beliefs.

Identifying Automatic Negative Thoughts (ANTs)

ANTs are those stark, negative knee-jerk reactions that pop into your head without any conscious effort. Examples include thoughts like "I'm not good enough" or "Nothing will ever change."

Tip: Name your thoughts. When you catch yourself having an ANT thought, label it for what it is not - a fact but a belief. Tell yourself, "That's just an idea" to help weaken its power.

The "STOP" Method: When an ANT enters your mind, mentally

say "STOP!" and take some time to consider whether that idea is truly helpful or accurate.

Challenging Unrealistic and Harmful Beliefs

Many negative thoughts are based on distorted or false beliefs about yourself or your situation. This is particularly important now.

Ask Questions of Yourself: "Is it really true?" When you notice a negative thought in your mind, ask yourself this question: "Is it really true?" or "What proof do I have to support this belief?" Quite often, the thought will be shown to be unverified.

Turning Negative Talk into Positive Constructive Dialogue

After spotting and questioning a negative thought, you should now replace it with something more constructive. Rather than let negative language capture you, move decisively in consciousness.

For instance, instead of saying "I always mess things up". Try something like, "sometimes things just don't work out, but that's OK. Every day, I am getting on with things and making a little progress, day by day."

Start Your Go-To List

Whenever negative thoughts arise, list those thoughts in a constructive manner. You can then refer to the list whenever you're feeling buried under negativity with a helpful and supportive answer.

Cognitive restructuring methods

Cognitive restructuring means changing the way you think to perceive situations more positively. The aim is to transform adverse interpretations into balanced, constructive ones.

Turn Problems into Opportunities

When things go wrong, rather than feeling, "This is dreadful," change your perspective to: "This is tough, but I can gain something from it." Thus, re-framing suffering as challenges allows you to take them on not as obstacles but as chances for growth.

"If-Then" Planning Strategies

Before negative thought patterns begin to alter your cognition, be sure that your mind knows to steer itself the other way. For example, if I should ever begin to have thoughts such as "this can't be done," I remind myself of previous challenges that were successfully completed. Through using these methods as support structures to struggle against doubt and confusion, you can proceed confidently into the future with a clear sense of direction.

Affirmations and empowerment strategies

Positive affirmations are powerful tools for reprogramming your mind and boosting confidence in yourself.

Tip: Formulate personalised affirmations. Rather than using generic affirmations like "I am strong", tailor them to your experiences. Instead of saying, "I always fail at this," try re-framing it to, "I'm working on improving, and each setback is a chance to learn and grow." This shift encourages a mindset of progress rather than defeat, helping you focus on development rather than limitations.

Tip: Visualise success. Dedicate a few minutes each day to imagine yourself navigating a challenging situation success-fully or experiencing the feeling of achieving a major victory. These visualisations reinforce the belief that positive change is achievable and help maintain a mindset focused on growth and success.

Gratitude as a Daily Practice

Gratitude can lift your focus from what's wrong in your life to what's right.

Tip: Launch a gratitude journal. Each day, jot down three things you were thankful for, no matter how small. With time and practise this habit will retrain your mind to see the positive things in life.

Tip: Activate gratitude reminders for yourself. If you feel stuck on coming up with anything, try these: "What's one thing that made me smile today?" or "What's something I tend to overlook but need to take time to appreciate?"

Skills for Regulating Emotions

Emotions, especially strong ones, are often like a runaway train: they seem very much in control. Emotion regulation means learning to recognise and manage one's emotions in a healthy way which does not become overwhelmed by them.

Understanding Emotional Triggers

Certain situations or people may provoke the most intense emotional reactions. Identifying these "triggers" is central to emotional regulation.

Tip: You can keep an emotion log. Next time you experience a strong emotion, jot down what happened, what you felt and any thoughts that arise. This will help you see patterns in your emotional responses.

Tip: Look back at situations in the past. Recall times when you felt extremely overwhelmed. What was going on? What triggered those feelings?

Sensitivity and Over reactivity Management

If you are someone who tends to overreact, it is crucial to handle your sensitivity. Practise "Pause and Breathe": Before you respond, take 3- slow deep breaths to quiet your reactions. Intense emotions make us susceptible to overreacting even to the smallest of things and that realisation is crucial so as not to impulsively react.

Coping Skills for Extreme Emotions

1- Box Breathing: Inhale for 4, hold for 4, exhale for 4 and hold it out for another 4. Keep doing this to relax your body and mind.

2- Sensory Anchoring: Pay attention to your senses—5 things you see, 4 things you can touch, 3 things you hear, 2 things you smell and 1 thing to taste.

3- Concentrate on Breathing: When you begin to feel stressed out, take the time out to focus on feeling your inhales and exhales.

4- Body Scan: Take a moment to get into your body by doing a scan of where you might be carrying tension in the present moment and toning down the overwhelm.

Emotional intelligence and emotional fortitude

Emotional intelligence refers to the ability to be aware of and comprehend both one's own emotions and those of others. Like any other skill it is developed with practice.

Tip: Understand your feelings. When you are experiencing a particularly strong emotion, take some time to call it what it is.

Tip: Realise that empathy is not a gift. When you are working with other people, you can try to take their feelings and perspectives into account. This leads to warm personal relationships and helps you navigate strife with much greater ease.

31

Developing Emotional Support Networks

You cannot heal from depression alone. You need to have other people to share your emotions and support you. This is very important for maintaining mental health.

Finding Safe Places to Talk About Your Pain

Having someone or someplace where you can feel secure in expressing your emotions can be a healing experience.

Tip: Identify your "safe people." Think of a few individuals in your life who are trustworthy listeners. This may be a close friend, family member, or therapist.

Tip: Look into peer Counselling groups. Finding others who have gone through similar experiences can provide comfort and validation. Many times, you can find these groups online or even face to face.

Counselling and Psychotherapy

Getting professional help is the key to people with depression and emotional challenges gaining the resources they need to cope.

Tip: Research various forms of therapy. Whether it is cognitive-behavioural therapy (CBT), counselling or group therapy, look for a style that suits you and meets your needs.

Tip: Don't be afraid to ask for help. If you are feeling stuck, overwhelmed, or anything else negative, a professional can give new viewpoints and strategies for dealing with things.

Expression for Release

Emotions are sophisticated; sometimes too complex or overwhelming to be expressed through words only. Creative outlets in these moments become more potent ways to channel energy, finding your way through into something new. Expressing yourself artistically or physically —via painting, writing, music and dance or making in general—provides a non-verbal intuitive way of processing emotions.

Whether it's producing a piece of art or jotting down a journal entry, putting something out there can be its own kind of stress relief. It converts inner turmoil into something concrete which enables you to think about the state of your emotions more strategically. In addition, these artistic activities create empowerment and offer an outlet for emotions; a way of releasing some emotional stress and aiding the process of recovery.

Not only does the expression of emotions release them but also, creative outlets are an opportunity for true self-discovery and growth. By looking at the way you communicate in an artistic manner, such as expressing yourself through writing, painting or movement you begin to see certain patterns that unfold greater insights into your emotions and experiences which can lead to a deeper self-awareness and emotional resilience.

Tip: Seek out groups of like-minded people. Whether it's a book club, sports club or online community, joining a group with common interests can help you feel part of something bigger than yourself.

Tip: Don't fall into isolation. If you notice that your habits are changing and you're withdrawing from people, try to reach out.

Taming your emotions and running your own thoughts is a skill that requires practice. Yet out of these strategies, you can find yourself better able to cope with life's ups and downs. Always remember, each small step in this direction makes your life that much more balanced and abundant.

4

Chapter 4: Living Beyond Depression

T his chapter looks at practical strategies for creating the kind of life that gives you a thrill, preserving your emotional balance over time, and a good relationship with yourself. We'll break these down one by one with specific measures to help you survive and thrive.

Making the Life You Want

Getting past depression involves rediscovering the things that make life worth living. It is about intentionally constructing a life in which you are enthusiastic about everything you do — where your days are filled with activities that "fit" who and what you are deeply committed to. Here is how to begin.

Identifying Passions and Interests

Go back over the things you used to do. What brought you joy as a child or young person? Whether it was painting or writing, playing a sport or being outdoors in nature, reviving old hobbies can once more bring light into your life.

Actionable Tip: Choose one day a week for a "passion hour" when you can explore or revive some activity that once gave you pleasure. Start small — it might mean reading only a chapter of something you like or making a sketch for a quarter-hour.

Recovering Hobbies and Activities

Don't force yourself to pick up everything you did before. Take your own time to learn what activities now truly speak to your heart. Some past hobbies may no longer feel as enjoyable as others, and that's perfectly okay.

Actionable Tip: Write down five hobbies you once liked and set out to reintroduce each of them separately during the next few months. Look how each one makes you feel— keep those that give happiness.

Exploring new experiences and interests

It is during this time of recovery that you will wish to try new things without hesitation. Join a local club/group, take classes in some hobby you enjoy or take up a new one. Looking into different interests can open doors to hobbies you never even knew existed in your heart.

Actionable Tip: Every month, challenge yourself to DO something new. Maybe try making an entirely different recipe that you've never made before; sign up for a fitness class; go on a trip to some place you haven't been before - remember what those new things feel like and take note of them in your mind.

Creating Meaning Through Passion Projects

A passion project is a long-term goal or project that brings you joy and fulfilment. This might mean writing a blog, starting up a small sideline business or lending support to those causes close to your heart. One thing that feels significant in your life can be very nourishing.

Actionable Tip: Start small with 30 minutes each week on a passion project. Gradually, as you get into the habit and build momentum, increase this time.

Setting Long-term Goals for Happiness

The long-term goals are stepping-stones to the life you want. Begin by envisioning what makes you most happy. Where will you be in five or ten years, and with what kind of people around? What kind of life will fulfil success for yourself?

Actionable Tip: Break down big goals (career, personal or creative) into smaller, manageable steps. Say you want to change careers, lay out small milestones such as researching new fields of work, taking courses needed for that field, and getting to know people who are involved in such work.

Building a Roadmap for Continued Happiness

It's easy to forget how far you've come without some sort of plan. But creating a road map — a visual plan with timelines — helps to keep your nose to the grindstone and measures just what successes are being achieved in each phase.

Realistic Advice: Outline clear long-term goals in a goal-setting journal or app. Assess your progress monthly but more importantly concentrate on areas that need improvement.

Make Long-Term Goal Mapping a Priority: Try to always waive fewer clear-cut targets and build them. Review your month- At the end of every month, evaluate your progress. Use this tool, for example, to break the cycles of unhealthy habits.

Actionable Step: Make sure to have dedicated time for self-reflection. Tracking your emotional and mental health as part of a review (like a monthly or quarterly one) can give you great personal growth insights.

Begin to build a proactive self-care routine each day instead of reacting to stress on the fly. Practising some mindfulness, journaling or even just taking a few deep breaths for 5 minutes can hugely benefit your mental health.

How to stop a burnout: Balance is key. In your to do list, reserve some time during the day for relaxing. Just like a manager schedules breaks, it creates time for productivity as well as rest.

Developing A Positive Sense of Self

Be kind to yourself. As human beings, when things do not go our way which is completely natural, show yourself the same love and care you would a friend. This makes it easier to have a kinder relationship with yourself and allows for building sustainable self-confidence over time.

Actionable Tip: When you make a mistake, speak to yourself with kindness and practice self-compassion. Instead of saying "I'm a failure," say something like "I'm learning and that's okay!"

Forgiving Yourself for Past Mistakes

We all make mistakes, but carrying around guilt or regret will haunt us forever. Letting go of the past and even forgiving ourselves, this is an important part of the healing process.

Learning to Accept Imperfections

Perfectionism is poison to your mental health. Realising that you're imperfect—and that's normal—frees you from the need to live unauthentically.

Actionable Tip: To stop being perfectionists, start letting go by allowing yourself to make small mistakes without self-reproach.

For instance, if you make a slip-up in action, remind yourself that you are human and it's OK to make a mistake. Mistakes can be lessons!

Celebrating Personal Progress and Achievements

Celebrate how far you have come, even if the steps are small. Progress needs recognition.

Actionable Tip: Keep a "progress journal" where you write down small victories, no matter how insignificant they may be. Go back and read through it occasionally to remind yourself of your growth.

Staying Connected to Your Sense of Purpose

Living a purpose-driven life keeps you on track and motivated. Whether your life's mission is personal fulfilment or contributing to the wider world, it gives you direction.

Actionable Tip: Write a statement of purpose—a few sentences that describe what makes your life meaningful. Keep it in a place where you will see it every day and remember your "why."

Strategies for Long-Term Emotional Well-Being

Keeping yourself happy is a continuous process. It requires regular self-care, introspection, and the ability to adapt to different seasons in life.

Regular Self-Care and Mental Health Check-Ins

To learn what your emotional or mental state really is, ask yourself frequently how you're feeling. Self-care is not just bubble baths-it involves other deliberate acts of kindness towards yourself that support well-being.

Actionable Tip: Allocate 15 minutes per week "self-care check in" reflecting on your feelings. Ask yourself what more or less of those moments you need in the future.

Scheduling Time for Self-Reflection

Being in tune with yourself on a regular basis can help you stay away from any early warning signs of stress or overwhelm before they turn into bigger problems.

Actionable Tip: For self-reflection either keep a notebook at hand or meditate. You can jot down your thoughts in writing or take five minutes to meditate before work on your mood state now that you're aware of it.

Implementing Mental Health "Maintenance" Habits

Just as your physical health requires regular maintenance, so does your mental health. This means practices like being physically active and sustaining vibrant unions with others outside the family, as well as engaging in activities which nourish your soul.

Actionable Tip: Develop a schedule for the week which includes behaviour, connection with others and rest. For mental health maintenance, regular attention is needed. Have you started meditation yet?

Knowing When to Seek Support Again

Understand that help will be required at times, even after you have made progress. Knowing when to seek help can prevent emotional relapses

Actionable Tip: Be aware of any early warning signs that may suggest you need help, such as withdrawing from activities or feelings of being overwhelmed. When these signals emerge, contact a therapist or support system.

Practising Gratitude and Positivity

Gratitude provides an excellent method of shifting your mindset from concentrating on setbacks to seeing the joys in life.

Actionable Tip: Start a daily gratitude exercise by recording three items that have cheered you each day. This will help to lift your spirits and get more out of life.

Make sure that the environment is Healthy

The state of your well-being resembles that which you create within, both physically and psychologically. Negativity will hold you back, so getting beyond a place of depression means changing and moving forward. Clean your place, one room at a time (there's no rush), and make connections throughout your support system to better serve your own mental health.

Tip: Keep your living space clutter free and surround yourself with positivity. Avoid substance abuse, gambling or toxic relationships.

It will be easier to adopt a positive behaviour if you start doing these practices often. You can take the first step at home, which will bring peace to the mind.

Tip: Choose a specific afternoon to declutter an area of your home that seems daunting. Think about your bonds as well: Ditch those people that suck you dry and bolster the relationships that build you up.

Surviving depression is not merely stopping the misery, but rather to create a life that you naturally contribute to and always maintain an emotional health. And so, taking these practical steps will bring you one step closer to a life of fulfilment and joy.

5

Additional Support

H ere is a list of additional support if you are facing difficult times:

1. Samaritans

Phone: 116 123

Website: www.samaritans.org

Available 24/7, providing emotional support for anyone in distress or struggling to cope.

2. Mind

Phone: 0300 123 3393

Website: www.mind.org.uk

Offers information and support for mental health issues, including advice on where to find local services.

3. CALM (Campaign Against Living Miserably)

Phone: 0800 58 58 58

Website: www.thecalmzone.net

Support for men in the UK who are feeling down or in crisis.

4. *Shout*
   Text: 85258
   Website: www.giveusashout.org
   A free, confidential, 24/7 text messaging support service for anyone in crisis.

5. *Rethink Mental Illness*
   Phone: 0300 5000 927
   Website: www.rethink.org
   Provides advice, information, and support for those affected by mental illness.

6. *NHS Mental Health Services*
   Website: www.nhs.uk/mental-health
   Access NHS mental health services, including crisis support, therapy, and advice on mental health conditions.

7. *SANEline*
   Phone: 0300 304 7000 (available 4:30pm - 10:30pm daily)
   Website: www.sane.org.uk
   Provides emotional support and guidance for people affected by mental illness.

8. *Papyrus HOPELINEUK*
   Phone: 0800 068 4141
   Website: www.papyrus-uk.org
   Support for young people struggling with suicidal thoughts and emotional distress.

6

Conclusion

H *ere you are, and that's a real accomplishment. Living beyond depression isn't about getting through the moments*

of emptiness and sadness. It's about shaping a vision for the rest of your life that is bright, full of happiness and meaning. You've already taken some of the most important steps: facing your struggles, deciding to make change and studying to create the life you love.

Just remember, healing is not a destination but a journey lasting all your life. There will be ups and downs, moments of victory followed by moments of struggle. What counts is not that the road ahead isn't perfect, but that you keep on going with courage, resourcefulness and self-compassion.

As you move through this journey, remember every small step, whether it's finding new passions, setting goals that align with your values or simply being kinder to yourself, carries more great rewards than you can imagine. You're moving closer and closer to the person who can thrive, not just survive. Live and not just exist.

This book is meant to remind you that you are capable of change and your life is brimming with possibility. You have the strength to meet any challenge head on, and the wisdom to seek help when needed. Most importantly, you have the power to shape your own life, so it brings something meaningful, joyous and fulfilling.

Keep moving forward, taking pleasure in each little victory. Chart progress, no matter how gradual. Always remember that you deserve happiness and peace, and the life you want. The road to living beyond depression isn't always easy, but it brings great satisfaction. Believe in yourself and the process.

The best is yet to come. Keep at it. You can do it...

Thanks for reading all of this, and consciously taking the time to do so. I genuinely appreciate your dedication to take in the messages, and I hope that these insights and concepts have found meaning with you. You have already taken one step in understanding and growth by engaging until the end — and that is something you can recognise.

If you found value in this book, I would be very grateful if you could leave a review at Amazon. I would love to hear from you.

Epilogue

By now, as you finish reading this book, I trust that you have gained the tools and insights to help you start on the path of healing. The path you are on is a hard one, but every baby step (and even backwards steps) has been pulling you towards recovery inch by inch.

Healing from depression is not a place, healing from depression is a journey of always becoming and learning to be kind to yourself. Some days are great, and you feel that all is well with the world, other days though, that old weight tries to work its way back in. But now you know, that despite how it feels right now, you can control your emotions, change your thoughts and create a life where you are happy.

You have learned in this book how to make sense of your depression, how to master your thoughts, how to be good to yourself emotionally and physically, and how to build the life you most want. You realise that there can be light at the end of this tunnel, and setbacks are just a part of it. But like in most things, it is not the perfect score that counts as much as keeping on trying. All attempts are saved, and every little bit of self-care is a win.

You should finish this book feeling a deeper sense of empowerment. Yes, you can set the course for your own life and as I always say there will be some rough seas along the way, but now you too know how to sail with fortitude and hope.

Be sure to remember along the way that every achievement, no matter how little you think it might be, deserves celebrating. Be gentle with yourself and keep building on your foundation. You have greater potential than you can even imagine, and your power is in never giving up, when the road ahead seems dark.

Thank you for letting me join you on your journey. It has been my honour to have this opportunity for us to occupy the same space, and I hope that what you found in this book will help direct you towards something brighter and far more fulfilling.

You are not alone in this. There is always hope. Better days are coming.

With gratitude and hope,

Peter

Afterword

Before you close the last pages in this book, I want to pause to think about our time together. For the readers—whether you have read all the way through each chapter or just those that most resonated with you, I hope you feel more empowered, hopeful and connected in yourself and your journey of healing.

Depression is a personal and stubborn fight, one that takes patience and bravery, one that means we must keep pushing onwards even when everything feels like it is pulling us back. During that journey the book was penned as a companion — giving you insights, tools and strategies, motivation and most importantly the reminder that you are never alone in this.

Healing doesn't mean you will not experience difficulty, it means you have the power to overcome them.

If the processes I shared intrigued you, keep applying and practising them in your life and remember to always be kind to yourself- growth is a process. Life will have its ups and downs but with the knowledge that you now possess, you can cope with the bad times and relish in the good.

You are still in the process of healing, and I know that you can forge a life full of meaning, happiness, and tranquillity.

Thank you for letting me be a part of your journey, and I hope this book also becomes food for thought next time you cherish it. You are more powerful than you realise, and the future is completely up to you.

With deep gratitude,
Peter

About the Author

Born in Birmingham, Peter has dedicated his life to the magic of language to heal, link and create. Over a decade of experience in commercial and community theatre, with an impressive body of work. His passion for storytelling has translated into his writing, most notably with his successful theatre show titled 'Matt.'

Peter's commitment to developing and sharing creativity in the performing arts has resulted in much of his theatre work being community-focused, not only in East Anglia but across the UK, as well as Portugal and North Macedonia.

Peter loves to travel to other countries such as Cape Verde and Portugal and he likes to keep fit, focused and stay healthy by attending his local gym, going for jogs near the beach in his hometown that is now, Great Yarmouth. He loves 90's rap music and his favourite artist of all time is 2pac and his favourite movie is Wizard Of Oz. He also loves to play basketball and watch football where he supports Aston Villa.

You can connect with me on:

- 🌐 https://reflectproductions.myshopify.com
- 🐦 https://x.com/reflecttheatre
- ⓕ https://www.facebook.com/MattAPieceOfTheatre
- 🔗 https://www.youtube.com/@reflect_theatre
- 🔗 https://www.instagram.com/reflecttheatre

Printed in Great Britain
by Amazon